Arts Of Miracle

By

Bimpe Gold-Idowu

Arts of Miracle

Copyright © 2021 by Bimpe Gold-Idowu.

All rights reserved. No part of this book may be reproduced or transmitted in any form or by any means without the written permission from the author or publisher.

Published by:

Ware Resources and Publishing
www.wareresources.com

1-888-469-4850 Ext. 2

ISBN 978-1-7360798-9-8
LCCN# 2022908963

Printed in USA by Ware Resources and Publishing

TABLE OF CONTENTS

INTRODUCTION	7
ETYMOLOGY OF MIRACLE	10-17
WHY DO WE NEED MIRACLE	18-22
EXISTENCE OF MIRACLE	23-26
MIRACULOUS OCCURRENCES	27
BARRENNESS TO FRUITFULNESS	27-30
STIGMA OF NAAMAN	30-35
FAMINE TO SURPLUS	35-37
DEAD-END TO A CLEAR PATH	38-40
RISEN OF THE DEAD	40-43
TYPOLOGY OF MIRACLE	44-45
CHANNEL OF GRACE	46-57
CHANNEL OF FAITH	58-64
CHANNEL OF GOOD DEEDS	65-85
CHANNEL OF PERSISTENCE	85-90
CHANNEL OF SUPPLICATION	91-117
CHANNEL OF THANKSGIVING	118-124
GETTING THE RESULT	125-126
ACTIVATING THE MIRACLE	137-159

Introduction

After seeing many people running helter-skelter looking for miracle, searching for God when He is not lost. I felt pity welled up within me for their ignorance on looking for God when He is always near. Many have gone into diabolical means just to access miracle believing that it can only be obtained through occultism. Human has forgotten that with the creation of this world, it was by a miracle; through the Word the world and everything in it came into. Why then do we have to go out of the way to seek miracle when our Lord Jesus is the miracle Himself.

We have God the Father El-Shaddai whom is the All Possible, Jesus the Son whom is the Word and through Him we are created and the Holy Spirit who makes things come true with us. Having The Trinity with us, then why do we need to look for miracle elsewhere? When God comes down; miracle happens. When you have Jesus with you; you have Miracle with you because He cannot be with you and darkness with his host still stay with you. When you have Holy

Spirit as your Intercessor, miracle must surely take place because Holy Spirit will tender your case with God.

In Arts Of Miracle, we are going to be talking about Miracle and how to access it. Before getting a miracle for or asking for one, we must first know the typology of miracle in the spiritual realm. Some miracles are obtained by grace without asking for it, some by faith of the receiver, some through supplication, some by persistence and some by our good deeds. All miracles are visible but not all are touchable. Miracle comes in different forms.

This book will take you through the journey of miracle and if you desire, how to access, activate and getting the desired results then you will become a Miracle Carrier.

CHAPTER ONE

ETYMOLOGY OF MIRACLE

Everyone wants a miracle, either a believer or an atheist, we all crave for miracle consciously or unconsciously in every area of our lives. A student looking for a miracle on how to pass a very hard exam, career people looking for miracle in that difficult field that is so competitive, medics hoping for miracle is a difficult experiment, even a politician secretly praying for that miracle for a hopeless campaign, what about Ministers in the vineyard? Of course, we all pray for miracle to take place in the congregation when we mount the altar and brethren come to get a miracle from sickness, financial struggles, addictions with sin of the flesh. It goes on and on.

Before thinking about getting a miracle, let us go back in history, to the genesis of it all. What is miracle? How does it come about? Why do we need it? Does miracle really exist?

ETYMOLOGY OF MIRACLE

Miracle itself can be defined as Jesus, it comes from the spiritual name of God the son. According to today's definition, miracle is making the impossible possible. Getting a breakthrough for a hopeless situation or bringing a dream to reality. Miracle is always visible and perfect.

> *James 1:17 KJV*
> *"Every good gift and every perfect gift is from above, and cometh down from the Father of lights, with whom is no variableness, neither shadow of turning."*

But if Jesus is Miracle, how then do non-believers also receive miracle? Let us go back to the genesis of it all. Who is Jesus?

> *John 1:1-3 KJV*
>
> *"In the beginning was the Word, and the Word was with God, and the Word was God. The same was in the beginning with God. All things were made by him; and without him was not anything made that was made."*

Jesus is the Word, the creator of all things. Everything was made through him which means He created both believers and non-believers. The Bible made us to know that God The Father created everything both in heaven and in the earth by The Word which is Jesus; the incarnated Son Of God. When He created everything, they were all in good and perfect state.

> *1 Timothy 4:4 KJV*
>
> *"For every creature of God is good, and nothing to be refused, if it be received with thanksgiving"*

HOW DOES IT COMES ABOUT ?

God wishes to have a representative on earth who will supervise all his works hence the creation of man in the garden of Eden.

Genesis 2:4-8 KJVA
"These are the generations of the heavens and of the earth when they were created, in the day that the Lord God made the earth and the heavens, and every plant of the field before it was in the earth, and every herb of the field before it grew: for the Lord God had not caused it to rain upon the earth, and there was not a man to till the ground. But there went up a mist from the earth, and watered the whole face of the ground. And the Lord God formed man of the dust of the ground, and breathed into his nostrils the breath of life; and man became a living soul. And the Lord God planted a garden eastward in Eden; and there he put the man whom he had formed."

God loved man very much and was consigned for him. God the Father, Son and Holy Spirit decided to make man like God in nature and attributes. God is not a man to have earthly body, man earthly body comes from the soul God used in the creation of man. Through the Word everything was created, this means with the Word miracle happened.

Unfortunately man disobeyed God in the garden of Eden leading to sin and banishment from the garden. This banishment brought about tribulations to man because man now stays in the world were Satan the king of darkness resides.

Satan was an angel of God in heaven, guiding the throne of God and also the head of Choristers in heaven. He was made more beautiful than the rest of the angels. He began to think that he was special, even thought he was more powerful. Who knows, maybe more powerful than The Word; God The Son.

Satan decided to overthrown God the Son by placing his own throne above God the Son.

> *Isaiah 14:12-14 KJVA*
>
> *"How art thou fallen from heaven, O Lucifer, son of the morning! How art thou cut down to the ground, which didst weaken the nations! For thou hast said in thine heart, I will ascend into heaven, I will exalt my throne above the stars of God: I will sit also upon the mount of the congregation, in the sides of the north: I will ascend above the heights of the clouds; I will be like the Most High."*

After overthrowing The Word, He would then overthrow God The Father;The Almighty, after all he is the one guiding The Almighty from harm. Satan did not know that he was just a decoration by the throne. He thought to himself that for him to be responsible in guiding the throne of The Almighty, then he must be mighty himself. He planned a coup with some other angels he had deceived with his fine speech. But God who knows the thought of all, always makes rules to regulate everything to come. He is greater than all

> *John 10:29 KJV*
> *"My Father, which gave them me, is greater than all; and no man is able to pluck them out of my Father's hand."*

Satan started war in heaven to overthrow the government of The Trinity

> *Revelation 12:7-11 KJV*
> *"And there was war in heaven: Michael and his angels fought against the dragon; and the dragon fought his and angels, and prevailed not; neither was their place found any more in heaven. And the great dragon was cast out, that old serpent, called the Devil, and Satan, which deceive the whole world: he was cast out into the earth, and his angels were cast out with him.*

And I heard a loud voice saying in heaven, Now is come salvation, and strength, and the kingdom of our God, and the power of his Christ: for the accuser of our brethren is cast down, which accused them before our God day and night. And they overcame him by the blood of the Lamb, and by the word of their testimony; and they loved not their lives unto the death."

Yes, the war was fierce, but he forgot that Miracle resides there. The loyal angels and angels of Satan fought fiercely, to end the war Angel Michael used the blood of the Lamb, the blood of Jesus Christ that was poured on the cross of Calvary as a weapon to fight Satan himself. Satan could not stand this blood, so he was chased away from heaven with his hosts by the blood and down into the earth where man now resides making the earth resident for both man and host of darkness

WHY DO WE NEED MIRACLE

Where there is darkness there must surely be trouble, pain, destruction and sorrow. The only hope in getting a miracle is an encounter with Miracle Himself. We live in a fallen world full of sin. Adam and Eve disobedient to the commandment Of God already separated us from the fellowship with The Trinity. Our spiritual eyes have gone blind and worldly eyes have been activated. We see and aspire material things that do not uplift our spirit. Man falling state gave Satan power over man, to rule and torment as he wishes.

John 8:44 KJV

"Ye are of your father the devil, and the lusts of your father ye will do: he was a murderer from the beginning, and abode not in the truth, because there is no truth in him. When he speaketh a lie, he speaketh of his own: for he is a liar, and the father of it."

Satan is the hater of all good things, no good can come out of him. His government is of slavery and man has been taken captive where man cannot exercise his rights. Satan government is a government of compulsion, he forces his wishes on people. His yoke is heavy and his punishment leads to death. We are in a hopeless world and the only way out of the captivity is by miracle. If we want to get out of the bondage, then we need Jesus Christ to take us out of it.

John 3:16 KJV
"For God so loved the world, that he gave his only begotten Son, that whosoever believeth in him should not perish, but have everlasting life."

God does not want us to perish in the bondage of Satan that disobedience got us into, so He offered His Son as a ransom for our sin. The Son left His heavenly glory to be born as a man but right from the beginning to the end, He exhibited miracle.

Luke 1:26-38 KJV

"And in the sixth month the angel Gabriel was sent from God unto a city of Galilee, named Nazareth, to a virgin espoused to a man whose name was Joseph, of the house of David; and the virgin's name was Mary. And the angel came in unto her, and said, Hail, thou that art highly favored, the Lord is with thee: blessed art thou among women. And when she saw him, she was troubled at his saying, and cast in her mind what manner of salutation this should be. And the angel said unto her, Fear not, Mary: for thou hast found favor with God. And, behold, thou shalt conceive in thy womb, and bring forth a son, and shalt call his name JESUS. He shall be great, and shall be called the Son of the Highest; and the Lord God shall give unto him the throne of his father David: and he shall reign over the house of Jacob forever; and of his kingdom there shall be no

end. Then said Mary unto the angel, How shall this be, seeing I know not a man? And the angel answered and said unto her, The Holy Ghost shall come upon thee, and the power of the Highest shall overshadow thee: therefore also that holy thing which shall be born of thee shall be called the Son of God. And, behold, thy cousin Elisabeth, she hath also conceived a son in her old age; and this is the sixth month with her, who was called barren. For with God nothing shall be impossible. And Mary said, Behold the handmaid of the Lord; be it unto me according to thy word. And the angel departed from her."

A virgin became pregnant without the seed of man and gave birth to a son. His pregnancy was a miracle which science could not comprehend still. His pregnancy was not through man and woman sexual intercourse making Him a divine being, while His birth by a woman gave Him man's body, nature and attributes. He became both God and man which made Him to feel pain like man and still perform miracle like God. He lived like a man on earth, eat, drink, sleep, even felt pain like we do. Satan waged war with Him when He was on earth, inciting people against Him. Satan made men crucified Jesus unawares of the plan of God. But by Jesus pain and death, He overpowered pain, sickness, sorrow and death for man.

Isaiah 53:4-5 KJVA

"Surely he hath borne our griefs, and carried our sorrows: yet we did esteem him stricken, smitten of God, and afflicted. But he was wounded for our transgressions, he was bruised for our iniquities: the chastisement of our peace was upon him; and with his stripes we are healed."

And by His resurrection, He reign over death. His victory over death set us at liberty from Satan. But this victory can only be accessed if we are His people.

EXISTENCE OF MIRACLE

Does miracle still exist? Of course it does. God The Father, Son and Holy Spirit was in the beginning, now and will always be. God is known as The Unchangeable God. Wherever God is, He speaks the Word and miracle happens. From time in memorial, miracle have been recorded to take place. The existence of God alone proof to us that there is miracle. Starting from Ontology; human idea of His Being. To Cosmology; shape of the world. Down to Geography; existence of animals in the world simultaneously even the Teleological argument; the design of the universe from the artistic point of view. All these lead to a supernatural Being, a Self-existence Being whom all derive their existence from. For such Being to sustain all, it can only be called Miracle; something extraordinary.

In the beginning of the world and existence of man, God fellowship with man in the garden of Eden and man was a miracle carrier then. Man lived with animals then and they did not harm man. Adam was in control of the beast then this was miracle in action. But after the fall of man, man stopped performing miracle. Man was created to be dependent on God but dependency of man is voluntary. Man can choose to depend on God or go the other way and depend on the devil. It is a two-way thing, either you choose God or Satan, no one is allowed to stay in the middle.

> *Matthew 12:30 KJV*
>
> *"He that is not with me is against me; and he that gathereth not with me scattereth abroad."*

God still cares for man so He began interacting with some certain people in the Old, these people are His chosen vessels. They became carriers of Miracle, by word from them, miracle happened. As humans multiplied on earth, God The Father decided to send His Son to us, when The Son arrived, He was God and man with human. By that human have Miracle with them. After His death, hope was almost lost, but alas, He resurrected and ascended into heaven leaving the promise of a Comforter. He promised to send another One like Him, who will teach us all things.

> *John 14:16-18 KJV*
>
> *"And I will pray the Father, and he shall give you another Comforter, that he may abide with you forever; Even the Spirit of truth; whom the world cannot receive, because it seeth him not, neither knoweth him: but ye know him; for he dwelleth with you, and shall be in you. I will not leave you comfortless: I will come to you.*

After the ascension of Jesus Christ back to heaven, The Comforter came

> *Acts 2:1-4 AMP*
>
> *"When the day of Pentecost had come, they were all together in one place, and suddenly a sound came from heaven like a rushing violent wind, and it filled the whole house where they were sitting. There appeared to them tongues resembling fire, which were being distributed*

[among them], and they rested on each one of them [as each person received the Holy Spirit]. And they were all filled [that is, diffused throughout their being] with the Holy Spirit and began to speak in other tongues (different languages), as the Spirit was giving them the ability to speak out [clearly and appropriately]."

The arrival of the Comforter was a miracle and immediately He descended on the disciples in the upper room, they all began to speak different languages, languages they have never learnt. This was a great miracle. The Holy Spirit now dwell in man, teaching us the ways of God. Man is now a carrier of miracle. Sadly, most do not realize that they carry miracle, through them miracle can be performed. What man only need to make miracle happens is by the activation of it.

In the next chapter, we will be looking at miraculous occurrence in the Bible and applying them to our lives.

CHAPTER TWO
MIRACULOUS OCCURRENCES

The Bible is the greatest and most concrete historical archive in world memorial. No record can beat that of the Holy Bible. As Christians, we will be looking into events in the Bible where miracles happened pertaining to lives of people seeking miracles from God.

BARRENNESS TO FRUITFULNESS

Abraham and Sarah

James 2:23 KJV

"And the scripture was fulfilled which saith, Abraham believed God, and it was imputed unto him for righteousness: and he was called the Friend of God."

Abraham was a friend of God, yet he suffered childlessness for a longtime because he was living in an imperfect world. He seek the face of God for a miracle and God answered his prayer, giving him a promise of a son.

> Genesis 13:14-16 AMP
> "The LORD said to Abram, after Lot had left him, "Now lift up your eyes and look from the place where you are standing, northward and southward and eastward and westward; for all the land which you see I will give to you and to your descendants forever. I will make your descendants [as numerous] as the dust of the earth, so that if a man could count the [grains of] dust of the earth, then your descendants could also be counted."

After waited for a longtime, he grew weary of the fulfillment of God's promise. His wife Sarah who was also getting old advised him to seek an alternative route to his situation. This is also what believers face when in a hopeless situation. We forget the God we have and His promise, listening to advice of man in place of God's own and forsaken God's way. Abraham listened to Sarah his wife and went in with his wife's maid. He got her pregnant but the child she begat was not the will of God for Abraham. The child was only the will of Abraham and Sarah, a child Sarah later grew to despise. Abraham went back to God to rededicate his ways to God and God in His infinite mercy accepted him back then reestablish His Love with Him.

> *Genesis 18:9-14 KJV*
>
> *"And they said unto him, Where is Sarah thy wife? And he said, Behold, in the tent. And he said, I will certainly return unto thee according to the time of life; and, lo, Sarah thy wife shall have a son. And Sarah heard it in the tent door, which was behind him. Now Abraham and Sarah were old and well stricken in age; and it ceased to be with Sarah after the manner of women. Therefore Sarah laughed within herself, saying, After I am waxed old shall I have pleasure, my lord being old also? And the Lord said unto Abraham, Wherefore*

did Sarah laugh, saying, Shall I of a surety bear a child, which am old? Is anything too hard for the Lord? At the time appointed I will return unto thee, according to the time of life, and Sarah shall have a son."

Although Abraham and Sarah were already old but God's covenant was not old and weary. Sarah had reached menopause where as a woman cannot conceive and bear a child again according to human science, but in God's science, her time is just ripe for child bearing. At ninety years of age, Sarah brought forth a son, by that time Abraham was one hundred years old already. Both of them were already forgotten by friends and relatives to nurse a child but God still has them in His plan. A plan for a miracle.

STIGMA OF NAAMAN

2 Kings 5:1 KJV
"Now Naaman, captain of the host of the king of Syria, was a great man with his

master, and honourable, because by him the Lord had given deliverance unto Syria: he was also a mighty man in valour, but he was a leper."

Naaman was a great captain in the host of the King of Syria, rich and powerful but there is a stigma in him; leprosy, a disease incurable during his time. He was in an impossible situation, he can only be cured through something divine.

2 Kings 5:3-11 KJV
"And she said unto her mistress, Would God my lord were with the prophet that is in Samaria! for he would recover him of his leprosy. And one went in, and told his lord, saying, Thus and thus said the maid that is of the land of Israel. And the king of Syria said, Go to, go, and I will send a letter unto the king of Israel. And he departed, and took with him ten talents of silver, and six thousand pieces of gold, and ten changes of raiment. And he

brought the letter to the king of Israel, saying, Now when this letter is come unto thee, behold, I have therewith sent Naaman my servant to thee, that thou mayest recover him of his leprosy. And it came to pass, when the king of Israel had read the letter, that he rent his clothes, and said, Am I God, to kill and to make alive, that this man doth send unto me to recover a man of his leprosy? wherefore consider, I pray you, and see how he seeketh a quarrel against me. And it was so, when Elisha the man of God had heard that the king of Israel had rent his clothes, that he sent to the king, saying, Wherefore hast thou rent thy clothes? let him come now to me, and he shall know that there is a prophet in Israel. So Naaman came with his horses and with his chariot, and stood at the door of the house of Elisha. And Elisha sent a messenger unto him, saying, Go and wash in Jordan seven times, and thy flesh shall come again to thee, and thou shalt be clean. But Naaman was wroth, and went away, and said, Behold, I thought, He will surely come out to me, and stand, and call on the name of the Lord his God, and strike his hand over the place, and recover the leper."

Naaman thought Elisha will come outside to meet him after hearing his name, to come and shake the whole earth for his sake but Elisha did not even come out to attend to him. What Elisha sent was Word to him because by himself he had no power to cure Naaman of his leprosy but he knows someone who can cure Naaman of his disease. Elisha knew that only God can cure him of his disease, so he sent him the Word Of God that was revealed to him; bathing in the river for seven times. The divine cure.
Naaman was angry because of his pride, he never taught Elisha would treat him like an ordinary person. He wanted to buy miracle with his status.

Romans 2:11 KJV
"For there is no respect of persons with God."

God does not look at our earthly status before showing mercy on us. He shows mercy to whoever He wishes.

> *Romans 9:15-16 KJV*
>
> *"For he saith to Moses, I will have mercy on whom I will have mercy, and I will have compassion on whom I will have compassion. So then it is not of him that willeth, nor of him that runneth, but of God that sheweth mercy."*

Naaman went to take the bath grudgingly, his mind was just half way in it, he was irritated but the Word Of God must surely come to pass.

> *Isaiah 55:10-11 KJV*
>
> *"For as the rain cometh down, and the snow from heaven, and returneth not thither, but watereth the earth, and maketh it bring forth and bud, that it may give seed to the sower, and bread to the eater: So shall my word be that goeth forth out of my mouth: it shall not return*

unto me void, but it shall accomplish that which I please, and it shall prosper in the thing whereto I sent it."

It has been spoken so it must take place, what Naaman only needed to do was to take action which he did and it ended in miracle. Elisha did not lay his hand on him to pray fervently for him rather he sent Word to him, remember Jesus is the Word. Naaman went to the river with the Word which is Jesus Christ and he got the miracle he seek for.

FAMINE TO SURPLUS

There was a great famine in Samaria as a result of the siege around it by the Syrians. None could come in or go out till the Samaritan exhausted their supplies. The people of the city has no other means of survival, so two Samaritan mothers deliberated among themselves and decided to use their children as meals in order to sustain themselves. Imagine such desperation.

2 Kings 6:24-29 KJV

"And it came to pass after this, that Ben-hadad king of Syria gathered all his host, and went up, and besieged Samaria. And there was a great famine in Samaria: and, behold, they besieged it, until an ass's head was sold for fourscore pieces of silver, and the fourth part of a cab of dove's dung for five pieces of silver. And as the king of Israel was passing by upon the wall, there cried a woman unto him, saying, Help, my lord, O king. And he said, If the Lord do not help thee, whence shall I help thee? out of the barnfloor, or out of the winepress? And the king said unto her, What aileth thee? And she answered, This woman said unto me, Give thy son, that we may eat him to day, and we will eat my son to morrow. So we boiled my son, and did eat him: and I said unto her on the next day, Give thy son, that we may eat him: and she hath hid her son."

Samaria needed extraordinary influence to overthrown the powerful Syrian King Ben-hadad II. There was no solution to the calamity, even the Samaria King was weakened already for he had to lean on a man for support. The only solution for them is to get someone who can plead to the supernatural force for assistance. Elisha was summoned by the King for he is their only hope for survival. With Word from God, Elisha prophesied

> *2 Kings 7:1 KJV*
> *"Then Elisha said, Hear ye the word of the Lord; Thus saith the Lord, Tomorrow about this time shall a measure of fine flour be sold for a shekel, and two measures of barley for a shekel, in the gate of Samaria."*

The prophecy seemed impossible to achieve, still it came to pass. Famine was turned to surplus without the Samaritan lifting a finger.

DEAD END TO A CLEAR PATH

After the Israelites managed to escape from the Egyptians captivity with God's help sending different plagues to the Egyptians. The Israelites were stuck at the Red Sea unable to crossover to the other side. On the other hand, the Egyptians were about to destroy them for leaving their land. Israelites were confused and afraid for their lives so they cried to Moses, who in turn cried out to God for deliverance from the hand of the Egyptians.

> *Exodus 14:11-14 KJV*
>
> *"And they said unto Moses, because there were no graves in Egypt, hast thou taken us away to die in the wilderness? wherefore hast thou dealt thus with us, to carry us forth out of Egypt? Is not this the word that we did tell thee in Egypt, saying, Let us alone, that we may serve the Egyptians? For it had been better for us to serve the Egyptians, than that we should die in the wilderness. And Moses said unto the people, Fear ye not, stand still, and see the*

salvation of the Lord, which he will shew to you today: for the Egyptians whom ye have seen today, ye shall see them again no more forever. The Lord shall fight for you, and ye shall hold your peace."

God responded to Moses, He gave Moses instruction of what to do. God gave him authority over the sea, Moses was able to part the sea by the proclamation of God's Word and the sea hearken to the voice of Moses because it was an authority from God. The Israelites received their miracle and they walked on dry land.

Exodus 14:26-29 KJV

"And the Lord said unto Moses, Stretch out thine hand over the sea, that the waters may come again upon the Egyptians, upon their chariots, and upon their horsemen. And Moses stretched forth his hand over the sea, and the sea returned to his strength when the morning appeared; and the Egyptians fled against it; and the Lord overthrew the Egyptians in the

midst of the sea. And the waters returned, and covered the chariots, and the horsemen, and all the host of Pharaoh that came into the sea after them; there remained not so much as one of them. But the children of Israel walked upon dry land in the midst of the sea; and the waters were a wall unto them on their right hand, and on their left."

For a perfect miracle, things of the past must be overthrown. The Egyptians were overthrown into the sea and were never seen again by the Israelites. By an encounter of God's miracle, past problem will be solved and forgotten.

RISEN OF THE DEAD

It sounds impossible to get the dead to rise again. It is medically impossible for a 4-day corpse to be seen walking, talking and eating. In fact, it is absolutely impossible for a tree already been cut of to grow fruits again. But Jesus Christ did exactly that

John 11:17 KJV

"Then when Jesus came, he found that he had lain in the grave four days already."

For every miracle, there must be an appointed time, a place and a lesson to learn from it. Miracle is meant to bring glory unto God. Jesus tarry in coming to Lazarus when he was sick, he waited until Lazarus died. It was not that Jesus was not consigned for Lazarus whom was referred to as Jesus friend but Jesus Christ deliberately stayed back in order to show God's Power over death. He wanted us to know and see that nothing is impossible for God to do. Lazarus that was dead and his body was already decaying rose up. Jesus Christ did the impossible.

John 11:41-44 KJV

"Then they took away the stone from the place where the dead was laid. And Jesus lifted up his eyes, and said, Father, I thank thee that thou hast heard me. And I knew that thou

hearest me always: but because of the people which stand by I said it, that they may believe that thou hast sent me. And when he thus had spoken, he cried with a loud voice, Lazarus, come forth. And he that was dead came forth, bound hand and foot with graveclothes: and his face was bound about with a napkin. Jesus saith unto them, Loose him, and let him go."

Jesus rose Lazarus up with the sound of his voice, He restored the decaying body back to a fresh and glowing body. He did not ask for help from any doctor, man or spirit to bring back Lazarus to life, He merely spoke and it was done.

Miraculous event can only take place by the Word spoken. The Word is the Miracle, miracle manifest at the mention of the Word. The right word and on God's instruction.

In the next chapter we will be looking at the typology of Miracle, how they vary and how they came to be.

CHAPTER THREE

TYPOLOGY OF MIRACLE

Miracle comes in different forms but it is all from the same source. We should note that not everything that seems like wonder is miracle.

> *Matthew 24:24 KJV*
> *"For there shall arise false Christs, and false prophets, and shall shew great signs and wonders; insomuch that, if it were possible, they shall deceive the very elect."*

Magic is the look alike of Miracle, it is a make believe which is not real, it is demonic, a deceit and it is from the devil. It is carried out by ministers of darkness.

> *Matthew 7:15-20 KJV*
> *"Beware of false prophets, which come to you in sheep's clothing, but inwardly they are*

ravening wolves. Ye shall know them by their fruits. Do men gather grapes of thorns, or figs of thistles? Even so every good tree bringeth forth good fruit; but a corrupt tree bringeth forth evil fruit. A good tree cannot bring forth evil fruit, neither can a corrupt tree bring forth good fruit. Every tree that bringeth not forth good fruit is hewn down, and cast into the fire. Wherefore by their fruits ye shall know them."

A true miracle is divine with no string attached. It comes from God and only Him decides who to give.

In this chapter, we will be discussing different channels of miracle in the Bible. Types of miracle that come from the throne of God the Father, Son and Holy Spirit; the originator Of Miracle. Miracle has different forms it takes and different channels depending on the positioning of the individual with the supernatural at that moment.

CHANNEL OF GRACE

It is by the grace of God that we are alive and going about our daily lives. Likewise, it is by His grace that miracle is obtained. Some people received miracle in the past not because they asked for it, not because they work for it, but by God's grace they received miracle.

THE RESIGNED BLINDMAN

John 9:1 KJV
"And as Jesus passed by, he saw a man which was blind from his birth."

This man was on his own, never asked to be cured of his blindness, he had accepted his fate, he did not complain of his blindness nor cried out to Jesus for a miracle.

> *John 9:10-12 KJV*
>
> *"Therefore said they unto him, How were thine eyes opened? He answered and said, A man that is called Jesus made clay, and anointed mine eyes, and said unto me, Go to the pool of Siloam, and wash: and I went and washed, and I received sight. Then said they unto him, Where is he? He said, I know not."*

This man does not even know Jesus to be The Son Of God because he was not part of Jesus followers. He was only consigned about surviving in his state.

Some miracles are carried out to bring glory unto God's name irrespective of the person who received the miracle. God gives out freely to all human hoping to bring back the lost with His love.

> *John 9:2-7 KJV*
>
> *"And his disciples asked him, saying, Master, who did sin, this man, or his parents, that he was born blind? Jesus answered, Neither hath this man sinned, nor his parents: but that the*

works of God should be made manifest in him. I must work the works of him that sent me, while it is day: the night cometh, when no man can work. As long as I am in the world, I am the light of the world. When he had thus spoken, he spat on the ground, and made clay of the spittle, and he anointed the eyes of the blind man with the clay, And said unto him, Go, wash in the pool of Siloam, (which is by interpretation, Sent.) He went his way therefore, and washed, and came seeing."

This man had an encounter with Jesus unknowingly and received his miracle, a man born blind was made to see.

THE UNFRUITFUL BUSINESS

Let us also look at the case of Peter, John and James the boat.

> *Luke 5:3 AMP*
>
> *"He got into one of the boats, which was Simon's, and asked him to put out a little distance from the shore. And He sat down and began teaching the crowds from the boat."*

Peter never invited Jesus into his boat, him and his partner were there for their own business. They came to fish and not to be a cab for a preacher. There were other boats in the river on that day, but Jesus chose to enter the boat of Peter.

- A minister is called by God and not the other way round. Ministers are vessels unto God, He chooses the one He wants.

Jesus chose Peter out of all in the river. Peter on his own part did not grumble for his service rendered even though it may not be convenient for him. He humbly accepted Jesus into the boat and even agreed to drive a little further into the sea. Throughout the night, Peter's work had been unprofitable, he had been working with no results. He was a professional fisherman and yet he caught not fish until Jesus entered his boat.

> *Luke 5:4-7 AMP*
> *"When He had finished speaking, He said to Simon [Peter], "Put out into the deep water and lower your nets for a catch [of fish]." Simon replied, "Master, we worked hard all night [to the point of exhaustion] and caught nothing [in our nets], but at Your word I will [do as you say and] lower the nets [again]." When they had done this, they caught a great number of fish, and their nets were [at the point of] breaking; so they signaled to their partners in the other boat to come and help them. And they came and filled both of the boats [with fish], so that they began to sink."*

Peter received the grace of been selected for the Master's work and the Master's work is always profitable.

Colossians 3:23-24 AMP

"Whatever you do [whatever your task may be], work from the soul [that is, put in your very best effort], as [something done] for the Lord and not for men, knowing [with all certainty] that it is from the Lord [not from men] that you will receive the inheritance which is your [greatest] reward. It is the Lord Christ whom you [actually] serve."

God does not use and dump, appointment by grace must surely bring forth fruit. A sea that refuses to produce a single fish throughout the night later produce surplus with the command of Jesus Christ. Miracle by grace is by the command of God in whom He pleases.

GRASS TO GRACE

Obedeodom was an unwanted man in the society because he was of no use to the society except to bother them with his needs, he was one of the poorest in the city. His death would not have bothered anyone in the city, infact they would have felt relieved that he is finally gone.

2 Samuel 6:2-7KJV

(2) And David arose, and went with all the people that were with him, from Baale-judah, to bring up from thence the ark of God, whereupon is called the Name, even the name of the LORD of hosts that sitteth upon the cherubim. (3) And they set the ark of God upon a new cart, and brought it out of the house of Abinadab that was in the hill; and Uzzah and Ahio, the sons of Abinadab, drove the new cart. (4) And they brought it out of the house of Abinadab, which was in the hill, with the ark of God, and Ahio went before the ark. (5) And David and all the house of Israel played before the LORD with all manner of instruments made of cypress-wood, and with harps, and with psalteries, and with timbrels, and with sistra, and with cymbals. (6) And when they came to the threshing-floor of Nacon, Uzzah put

forth his hand to the ark of God, and took hold of it; for the oxen stumbled.(7) And the anger of the LORD was kindled against Uzzah; and God smote him there for his error; and there he died by the ark of God.

Bringing the ark of God into Jerusalem would have been a great joy to all the people of the city for David intended to unite the Israelite in a religious way by making Jerusalem the religious headquarter to all Israelites but he and the Priests forgot to follow the rules of carrying the Ark. The ark of God was supposed to be carried on the shoulder by the priests and not on cart which King David wanted to transport the Ark, he introduced innovation without first consulting God. Secondly, only Levites have the right to come near or touch the ark but Uzzah was not a Levite, no matter how a hospital staff can be, once the staff is not a doctor then he cannot be allowed to perform an operation on a patient else he will face persecution.

These violations resulted into the death of Uzzah but David and the others were still ignorant of these hence the Bible word

> *Hosea 4:6KJV "My people are destroyed for lack of knowledge: because thou hast rejected knowledge, I will also reject thee, that thou shalt be no priest to me: seeing thou hast forgotten the law of thy God, I will also forget thy children".*

Fear gripped them and the King thought of an alternative place to put the Ark, he no more see the Ark as the representative of God but as a representative of death. He did not want anything to do with it again. The problem now is where would they put it, everybody in the city are valuable so they thought of Obed-edom the Gitite. He was been used as an experiment, he may either die or live. It is a risk that can be carried out only on someone that his death would not have been a great impact.

> *2 Samuel 6:9-11KJV*
> *And David was afraid of the LORD that day, and said, How shall the ark of the LORD come to me?*
>
> *So David would not remove the ark of the LORD unto him into the city of David: but David carried it aside into the house of Obededom the Gittite.*
>
> *And the ark of the LORD continued in the house of Obededom the Gittite three months: and the LORD blessed Obededom, and all his household.*

The Ark that killed Uzzah was the same Ark that blessed Obed-edom. Obed-edom never asked for the Ark to be brought to his house, he does not even have what it takes to house the Ark of God in his house financially. If he was to be the one to ask for it, he would have been requested to build a great and beautiful house for the Ark and to also make provision for the animals to be sacrificed for the daily rituals but in his case, he found grace

> *2 Samuel 6:12KJV "And it was told king David, saying, The LORD hath blessed the house of Obededom, and all that pertaineth unto him, because of the ark of God. So David went and brought up the ark of God from the house of Obededom into the city of David with gladness"*

The Ark was brought unannounced, he housed the Ark in his humble house and cared for it in his own way he can and in return God used the Ark to elevate his status to the extent that the King went and brought the Ark from Obed-edom's house to his city in order to be blessed also like Obed-edom. The unwanted Ark became the sort after just because of the grace found in the life of Obed-edom.

CHANNEL OF FAITH

For miracle to be performed by someone, there must be a strong faith in you and for you to receive miracle, you have to have faith in the power of God. When you lack faith in the minister you see, it will be impossible to receive miracle from such. Miracle is carried out through God's representatives on earth. It goes in two ways; the carrier and the receiver. Both must be strong in faith, where there is doubt, miracle is hopeless.

James 1:6-7 KJV

"But let him ask in faith, nothing wavering. For he that wavereth is like a wave of the sea driven with the wind and tossed. For let not that man think that he shall receive any thing of the Lord."

THE INCURABLE MADE WHOLE

The woman with the issue of Blood was not a close friend of Jesus neither was she in the agenda of Jesus Christ. There was no preparation for her healing on that day but she had a strong faith in the healing power of Jesus Christ.

Matthew 9:20-22 KJV
"And, behold, a woman, which was diseased with an issue of blood twelve years, came behind him, and touched the hem of his garment: For she said within herself, If I may but touch his garment, I shall be whole. But Jesus turned him about, and when he saw her, he said, Daughter, be of good comfort; thy faith hath made thee whole. And the woman was made whole from that hour."

She trusted in the work of Jesus and her faith moved her to an encounter with Christ. She knew it may not be possible for her to meet Jesus one on one for the crowd is much. She did not need an appointment to see him, neither did she asked to be prayed for. She knew that Jesus Christ is the Miracle, all what she needed to do was to get herself into close contact with Jesus. It does not matter if Jesus does not recognize her but as long as she can touch His garment, she knew she would receive her miracle. She received miracle based on her faith.

AN UNSHAKABLE FAITH OF A CENTURION

Let us also look at the centurion's servant. This man had a faith like no other. He knew that his servant was dying, a matter of life and death but he did not panic. Anxiety brings fear and where there is fear, faith cannot work.

Luke 7:2-8 KJV
"And a certain centurion's servant, who was dear unto him, was sick, and ready to die. And when he heard of Jesus, he sent unto him the

elders of the Jews, beseeching him that he would come and heal his servant. And when they came to Jesus, they besought him instantly, saying, That he was worthy for whom he should do this: For he loveth our nation, and he hath built us a synagogue. Then Jesus went with them. And when he was now not far from the house, the centurion sent friends to him, saying unto him, Lord, trouble not thyself: for I am not worthy that thou shouldest enter under my roof: Wherefore neither thought I myself worthy to come unto thee: but say in a word, and my servant shall be healed. For I also am a man set under authority, having under me soldiers, and I say unto one, Go, and he goeth; and to another, Come, and he cometh; and to my servant, Do this, and he doeth it."

He did not fall and beg Jesus to come to his house even when Jesus offered, he did not get hysterical because he did not lose hope. He only asked Jesus to say a word from where Jesus was and he believed that it will come to pass.

> *Luke 7:9-10 KJV*
> *"When Jesus heard these things, he marvelled at him, and turned him about, and said unto the people that followed him, I say unto you, I have not found so great faith, no, not in Israel. And they that were sent, returning to the house, found the servant whole that had been sick."*

Jesus was moved by his faith and proclaimed the Word. The centurion's wish was fulfilled because of his faith in Christ Jesus. Surely with faith, you can move mountain.

MIRACULOUS WORK OF UNKNOWN DISCIPLE

Likewise in the case of this unknown disciple

> *Luke 9:49-50 KJV*
>
> *"And John answered and said, Master, we saw one casting out devils in thy name; and we forbad him, because he followeth not with us. And Jesus said unto him, Forbid him not: for he that is not against us is for us."*

This disciple was unknown to the twelve, he was not chosen directly by Jesus Christ to be among the twelve disciples in order to cast out demons but this person believed in Jesus. His faith in the work and name of Jesus moved him to command the demon. He was able to perform miracles by the name of Jesus.

> *Philippians 2:9-11 KJV*
>
> *"Wherefore God also hath highly exalted him, and given him a name which is above every name: That at the name of Jesus every knee should bow, of things in heaven, and things in earth, and things under the earth; And that every tongue should confess that Jesus Christ is Lord, to the glory of God the Father."*

You may not be an ordained Pastor, but when you believe in the finished work of Christ and you work in accordance with the ways of God, you then become a carrier of miracle.

CHAPTER FOUR

CHANNEL OF GOOD DEEDS

Everything we do in life either good or bad is noted. There is record of all our deeds. Just like Satan brings to remembrance our atrocities so does God brings to remembrance our love, kindness and mercy we show to others.

> *Matthew 5:7 KJV*
> *"Blessed are the merciful: for they shall obtain mercy.*

We will all receive according to your deed. No one will go unrewarded either good or bad. We should all be conscious of our deed because everything is being recorded.

Revelation 22:12 KJV

"And, behold, I come quickly; and my reward is with me, to give every man according as his work shall be."

Some can receive miracle by their deeds irrespective of their religion. The most important thing to God is your heart, when your heart is pure and clean, you receive the blessings, favor, even miracle from God in other to bring glory unto His name and draw others to His goodwill.

OUTPOURING OF THE HOLY SPIRIT ON A GENTILE

Acts 10:1-4 AMP

"Now at Caesarea [Maritima] there was a man named Cornelius, a centurion of what was known as the Italian Regiment, a devout man and one who, along with all his household, feared God. He made many charitable donations to the Jewish people, and prayed to

God always. About the ninth hour (3:00 p.m.) of the day he clearly saw in a vision an angel of God who had come to him and said, "Cornelius!" Cornelius was frightened and stared intently at him and said, "What is it, lord (sir)?" And the angel said to him, "Your prayers and gifts of charity have ascended as a memorial offering before God [an offering made in remembrance of His past blessings]."

This man was a gentle man but he was unaware of Jesus Christ when he came to earth. Cornelius never heard the teaching of Jesus Christ neither was he a Jew, so according to the law of Moses he does not deserve to be saved because he does not observe the rigid law of Judaism. He was a gentile according to the Jews is Rome but still God found him because he was pure.

Acts 10:22 AMP
"They said, "Cornelius, a centurion, an upright and God-fearing man well spoken of

by all the Jewish people, was divinely instructed by a holy angel to send for you to come to his house and hear what you have to say.""

Cornelius and his family knew that it pays to be good, he loved fellow beings, cared for them and never discriminated between humans. He loved all equally and these are what God requires of us.

1 Peter 1:15-16 AMP
"But like the Holy One who called you, be holy yourselves in all your conduct [be set apart from the world by your godly character and moral courage]; because it is written, "Y OU SHALL BE HOLY (set apart), FOR I AM HOLY.""

Cornelius and his family were neither circumcised according to the law of Moses nor baptized, a requirement to receive Holy Spirit but these people did receive Holy Spirit just by accepting Jesus Christ as their Lord and savior.

> *Acts 10:44-48 AMP*
>
> *"While Peter was still speaking these words, the Holy Spirit fell on all those who were listening to the message [confirming God's acceptance of Gentiles]. All the circumcised believers who came with Peter were amazed, because the gift of the Holy Spirit had been poured out even on the Gentiles. For they heard them talking in [unknown] tongues (languages) and exalting and magnifying and praising God. Then Peter said, "Can anyone refuse water for these people to be baptized, since they have received the Holy Spirit just as we did?" And he ordered that they be baptized in the name of Jesus Christ. Then they asked him to stay there for a few days.*

It was his good deeds that moved God to save him. God saw his heart and decided to show mercy unto him. Cornelius with his family underwent baptism of the heart, then they received Holy Spirit along with the gifts of the Spirit. They experience the outpouring of the Holy Spirit by receiving it in full and they began to speak in tongues right there.

DEAD PHILANTHROPIST AROSE

Let us also look at the case of Tabitha, a woman also called Dorcas in Greek. Tabitha who was known to be a good woman, virtuous and caring and full time of good deeds. She was a philanthropist who never withheld herself from helping people, relieving them of their burdens and putting smiles on many faces.

> Acts 9:36-39 AMP
> *"Now in Joppa there was a disciple named Tabitha, (which translated into Greek means Dorcas). She was rich in acts of kindness and charity which she continually did. During that time it happened that she became sick and*

died; and when they had washed her body, they laid it in an upstairs room. Since Lydda was near Joppa, the disciples, hearing that Peter was there, sent two men to him, urging him, "Come to us without delay." So Peter got up [at once] and went with them. When he arrived, they brought him into the upstairs room; and all the widows stood beside him, weeping and showing [him] all the tunics and robes that Dorcas used to make while she was with them."

Her good deeds did not go unnoticed, many lamented her death, many wanted to die with her, lots wept and pleaded to God to bring her back. It was the sorrowful state of these people that moved Peter, Peter and the other disciples too were not unaware of her good deeds. Tabitha was a disciple of Jesus Christ she was one of the Seventy or Seventy-two Jesus sent out for evangelism in Acts 10. Evangelism is not limited to preaching the word alone, it goes with charity. When people are relieved, they will listen to what you have to say. Dorcas was an evangelist to the core, sharing what God had blessed her with the poor in both financially and spiritually. Her good attributes moved Peter and he prayed to God to bring her back to live because she was highly needed by people. Miracle took place and she came back to live.

> *Acts 9:40-41 AMP*
> *"But Peter sent them all out [of the room] and knelt down and prayed; then turning to the body he said, "Tabitha, arise!" And she opened her eyes, and when she saw Peter, she sat up. And he gave her his hand and helped her up; and then he called in the saints (God's people) and the widows, and he presented her [to them] alive."*

Many rich ones die today and people are jubilating that their tormentors are gone. But this woman died and people are lamenting that their helper is gone. Tabitha good deeds brought her a miracle. Having a right mind with God and man, your miracle is certain.

ENTERTAINED ANGELS AND WAS RESCUED

Sodom where Lot was leaving with his family was already under the judgment of God which was destruction of everything there, both living and non living. It has already been passed by God so Lot and his family were all supposed to perish with the people of Sodom but Lot was a good man, a righteous man who feared God and love his fellow himan. Sitting at the gate of Sodom, Lot saw two men, unknown to him that they were angels but he knew that they were not of the people in that city by their appearance so he offered them a place to stay and entertained them

> *Genesis 19:1-2KJV*
> *1 And there came two angels to Sodom at even; and Lot sat in the gate of Sodom: and*

Lot seeing them rose up to meet them; and he bowed himself with his face toward the ground;

2 And he said, Behold now, my lords, turn in, I pray you, into your servant's house, and tarry all night, and wash your feet, and ye shall rise up early, and go on your ways. And they said, Nay; but we will abide in the street all night.

Lot knew that these two people were in danger of being assualted by the locals who engaged in all sorts of immoral attitudes, ao he decided to put these two men under his wings.

Gen 19:4-13KJV
4 But before they lay down, the men of the city, even the men of Sodom, compassed the house round, both old and young, all the people from every quarter:

5 And they called unto Lot, and said unto him, Where are the men which came in to thee this night? bring them out unto us, that we may know them.

6 And Lot went out at the door unto them, and shut the door after him,

7 And said, I pray you, brethren, do not so wickedly.

8 Behold now, I have two daughters which have not known man; let me, I pray you, bring them out unto you, and do ye to them as is good in your eyes: only unto these men do nothing; for therefore came they under the shadow of my roof.

9 And they said, Stand back. And they said again, This one fellow came in to sojourn, and he will needs be a judge: now will we deal worse with thee, than with them. And they pressed sore upon the man, even Lot, and came near to break the door.

10 But the men put forth their hand, and pulled Lot into the house to them, and shut to the door.

11 And they smote the men that were at the door of the house with blindness, both small and great: so that they wearied themselves to find the door.

12 And the men said unto Lot, Hast thou here any besides? son in law, and thy sons, and thy daughters, and whatsoever thou hast in the city, bring them out of this place:

13 For we will destroy this place, because the cry of them is waxen great before the face of the LORD; and the LORD hath sent us to destroy it.

Lot and his family were saved because of his good deed. He protected the angels of God from harm, unknowingly to him that he was confirming who he is to the angels and he was spared from destruction.

A PROPHET WAS HOUSED AND A CHILD WAS GIVEN

A good deed is never taken forgranted by God but this good deed must be sone with love and your reward is the satisfaction you get by seeing the relief on the face of the ine receiving the good deed and not in the thank you word you get in return from man.

The Shunamite woman in 2 Kings 4:8 never knew that through her hospitality toward the prophet of God that she would be getting a child. Her reason for helping was to relief the man of God from stress by asking her husband to helo get a place for the man of God to rest when passing, relax and eat then continue on his journey.

> *2 Kings 4:8-10 KJV*
>
> *8 And it fell on a day, that Elisha passed to Shunem, where was a great woman; and she constrained him to eat bread. And so it was, that as oft as he passed by, he turned in thither to eat bread.*
>
> *9 And she said unto her husband, Behold now, I perceive that this is an holy man of God, which passeth by us continually.*
>
> *10 Let us make a little chamber, I pray thee, on the wall; and let us set for him there a bed, and a table, and a stool, and a candlestick: and it shall be, when he cometh to us, that he shall turn in thither.*

God will not reciev an act of love from you without giving you back something more valuable. This woman has been barreness for a longtime but she did not let that to way her down, she did not become bitter because of a situation, she was full of love and consign for people saw. She was looking for how to extend better lives around her and how to make others live comfortablely. This resulted in her miracle.

> 2 King 4:11-17. KJV
>
> 11 And it fell on a day, that he came thither, and he turned into the chamber, and lay there.
>
> 12 And he said to Gehazi his servant, Call this Shunammite. And when he had called her, she stood before him.
>
> 13 And he said unto him, Say now unto her, Behold, thou hast been careful for us with all

this care; what is to be done for thee? wouldest thou be spoken for to the king, or to the captain of the host? And she answered, I dwell among mine own people.

14 And he said, What then is to be done for her? And Gehazi answered, Verily she hath no child, and her husband is old.

15 And he said, Call her. And when he had called her, she stood in the door.

16 And he said, About this season, according to the time of life, thou shalt embrace a son. And she said, Nay, my lord, thou man of God, do not lie unto thine handmaid.

17 And the woman conceived, and bare a son at that season that Elisha had said unto her, according to the time of life.

Her good deeds was never forgotten, even when Satan wanted to steal her joy again by striking the child dead, God woke the child up for it is written:

> Matthew 5:7 KJV
> *Blessed are the merciful: for they shall obtain mercy.*

She showed mercy to the man of God by honouringGod and His annointing in Elisha's life and God gave her a miracle.

GAVE OUT LITTLE AND RECEIVE BOUNTIFULLY

Kindness is not on how much you give out or by your financial worth but kindness is being weigh on what manner you give and with what heart. You may give out millions but be considered stingy by God and you may give out little and be considered kind. Giving out should not be grudgingly but cheerfully and according to your capacity. This widow of Zarephath has been reduced to a financially poor woman probably by the famine in the land but she was still rich in the heart.

> *1 Kings 17:10-12 KJV*
> ***10*** *So he arose and went to Zarephath. And when he came to the gate of the city, behold, the widow woman was there gathering of sticks: and he called to her, and said, Fetch me, I pray thee, a little water in a vessel, that I may drink.*
>
> ***11*** *And as she was going to fetch it, he called to her, and said, Bring me, I pray thee, a morsel of bread in thine hand.*
>
> ***12*** *And she said, As the LORD thy God liveth, I have not a cake, but an handful of meal in a barrel, and a little oil in a cruse: and, behold, I am gathering two sticks, that I may go in*

and dress it for me and my son, that we may eat it, and die.

She had little and feared for what may become of her and her child still ahe did not let out her fustration and anger on Elijah. Elijah did not ask her to give him all the meal but out of it. She planned to divide the meal between her and her child but Elijah asked her to divide it among the three of them, HIM first, then HER and HER SON but she should make his first because of the level of his hunger. If she was a greedy and cruel hearted woman, she would have insulted the man of God or chased him away from her house but she did according to what he asked, she prepared his part first

1 Kings 17:14-17KJV
3 And Elijah said unto her, Fear not; go and do as thou hast said: but make me thereof a

little cake first, and bring it unto me, and after make for thee and for thy son.

__14__ For thus saith the LORD God of Israel, The barrel of meal shall not waste, neither shall the cruse of oil fail, until the day that the LORD sendeth rain upon the earth.

__15__ And she went and did according to the saying of Elijah: and she, and he, and her house, did eat many days.
__16__ And the barrel of meal wasted not, neither did the cruse of oil fail, according to the word of the LORD, which he spake by Elijah.

__17__ And it came to pass after these things, that the son of the woman, the mistress of the house, fell sick; and his sickness was so sore, that there was no breath left in him.

Alas, the other part of the flour never wasted nor did the oil dried off, her good deed resulted in her recieving a miracle and she and her household lived a comfortable lives.

CHANNEL OF PERSISTENCE

Some works are not done in a day or in the moment we seek them, likewise some miracles are not received instantly when we ask but by our persistent asking from God, we will receive it. Jesus Christ made this known that persistence pays off.

THE PERSISTENT WIDOW AND A JUDGE

> *Luke 18:1-8 KJV*
> *"And he spake a parable unto them to this end, that men ought always to pray, and not to faint; Saying, There was in a city a judge, which feared not God, neither regarded man:*

And there was a widow in that city; and she came unto him, saying, Avenge me of mine adversary. And he would not for a while: but afterward he said within himself, Though I fear not God, nor regard man; Yet because this widow troubleth me, I will avenge her, lest by her continual coming she weary me. And the Lord said, Hear what the unjust judge saith. And shall not God avenge his own elect, which cry day and night unto him, though he bear long with them? I tell you that he will avenge them speedily. Nevertheless when the Son of man cometh, shall he find faith on the earth?"

Just like a broker, you do not hit the target in just a day but by continuous work. Along the line, many will frustrate your effort, many will give you the negative signal, some will even ridicule your idea but still a good broker will remain positive and persistent. This widow made up her mind to get the just judgement either she is rich or not and the judge too had no choice that's to do her wish or else she will continue to pester his life. When you need a miracle, you keep up the faith and keep asking.

THE UNDERSERVED SYROPHOENICIAN WOMAN

Mark 7:25-31 KJV

"For a certain woman, whose young daughter had an unclean spirit, heard of him, and came and fell at his feet: The woman was a Greek, a Syrophoenician by nation; and she besought him that he would cast forth the devil out of her daughter. But Jesus said unto her, Let the children first be filled: for it is not meet to take the children's bread, and to cast it unto the dogs. And she answered and said unto him, Yes, Lord: yet the dogs under the table eat of the children's crumbs. And he said unto her, For this saying go thy way; the devil is gone out of thy daughter. And when she was come to her house, she found the devil gone out, and her daughter laid upon the bed. And again, departing from the coasts of Tyre and Sidon, he came unto the sea of Galilee, through the midst of the coasts of Decapolis."

This woman did not mind the insults or attitude shown, she took it all in as long as she would get what she needed. Jesus telling her Off was to see if she would faint in her request or if she would still keep to her request. Jesus wanted to see how long she would be able to go and how she would be able to take.

Most people do not last long on a mission once blockade shows up on the road, when antagonist waylay them, when difficulties are up ahead. Most preferred the easy road to success, where they are treated nicely, respected and recognized. This woman in response to Jesus was humble and respectful, she spoke nicely as if she was a friend and family. As a result, she received her miracle.

BARTIMAEUS THE BLIND

The blind man by the road side could have remained blind for the rest of his life, but he chose not by his persistent calling on Jesus the Son Of David to have pity on him.

Luke 18:35-36, 38-39 AMP

"As He was approaching Jericho [on His way to Jerusalem], it happened that a blind man was sitting beside the road begging. Now when he heard a crowd going by, he began to ask what this was [about].

So he shouted out, saying, "Jesus, Son of David (Messiah), have mercy on me!" Those who were leading the way were sternly telling him to keep quiet; but he screamed all the more, "Son of David, have mercy on me!""

People tried to shut him down coupled with lots of noise coming from the crowd, but all these did not deter him from calling out. Instead of him shutting up and loosing hope, he increased his voice in order to be heard. He knew that he either attract Jesus attention and be cured or succumbed to the pressure of people by keeping quiet and remain blind for the rest of his life. But he chose the former

Luke 18:40-43 AMP

"Then Jesus stopped and ordered that the blind man be led to Him; and when he came near, Jesus asked him, "What do you want Me to do for you?" He said, "Lord, let me regain my sight!" Jesus said to him, "Regain your sight; your [personal trust and confident] faith [in Me] has made you well." Immediately he regained his sight and began following Jesus, glorifying and praising and honoring God. And all the people, when they saw it, praised God."

His persistent calling later paid off and he received his miracle.

To go mile, you have to summon your courage and to go many miles, you have to be persistent. That is when you will achieve your aim and receive your miracle.

CHAPTER FIVE

CHANNEL OF SUPPLICATION

Prayer is our avenue to tender our request to God, during prayer we ask for what we need.

> *Matthew 7:7-11 AMP*
> *"Ask and keep on asking and it will be given to you; seek and keep on seeking and you will find; knock and keep on knocking and the door will be opened to you. For everyone who keeps on asking receives, and he who keeps on seeking finds, and to him who keeps on knocking, it will be opened. Or what man is there among you who, if his son asks for bread, will [instead] give him a stone? Or if he asks for a fish, will [instead] give him a snake? If you then, evil (sinful by nature) as you are, know how to give good and advantageous gifts to your children, how much more will your Father who is in heaven [perfect as He is] give*

what is good and advantageous to those who keep on asking Him."

Jesus Christ teaches that we should ask in humbles of heart inline with the will of God

Hebrews 4:16 AMP
"Therefore let us [with privilege] approach the throne of grace [that is, the throne of God's gracious favor] with confidence and without fear, so that we may receive mercy [for our failures] and find [His amazing] grace to help in time of need [an appropriate blessing, coming just at the right moment]."

SCARCITY TO SUFFICIENCY

Through prayer, the impossible is made possible. Even the disciples of our Lord Jesus did not know that many mouths could be fed with so little they had,

Luke 9:12-17 AMP

"Now the day was ending, and the twelve [disciples] came and said to Him, "Send the crowd away, so that they may go into the surrounding villages and countryside and find lodging, and get provisions; because here we are in an isolated place." But He said to them, "You give them something to eat." They said, "We have no more than five loaves and two fish—unless perhaps we go and buy food for all these people." (For there were about 5,000 men.) And He said to His disciples, "Have them sit down to eat in groups of about fifty each." They did so, and had them all sit down. Then He took the five loaves and the two fish, and He looked up to heaven [and gave thanks] and blessed them, and broke them and kept giving them to the disciples to set before the crowd. They all ate and were [completely] satisfied; and the broken pieces which they had left over were [abundant and were] picked up—twelve baskets full."

These disciples did not bother to feed the people because they were too much to be fed. All they had was five loaves of bread and two fishes, that certainly would not do for the multitude with them. Other solution would have been for them to go to the nearby settlement to buy food but Jesus Christ was with them. He demanded they be fed, He created everything when in heaven as God the Son, He still has His power to bring out whatever He wishes and He made it come into.

Jesus Christ made us to understand that by this act, prayer multiplies. With prayer, little can become plenty.

DESCEND OF THE HOLY SPIRIT

Acts 2:1 KJV
"And when the day of Pentecost was fully come, they were all with one accord in one place."

The Apostles did not just gather in that hour doing nothing, they were neither sleeping nor lazing around, they were praying in unity. Their prayer shook the foundation of the house they were and the presence of the Holy Spirit was felt.

Acts 2:2-8 KJV

"And suddenly there came a sound from heaven as of a rushing mighty wind, and it filled all the house where they were sitting. And there appeared unto them cloven tongues like as of fire, and it sat upon each of them. And they were all filled with the Holy Ghost, and began to speak with other tongues, as the Spirit gave them utterance. And there were dwelling at Jerusalem Jews, devout men, out of every nation under heaven. Now when this was noised abroad, the multitude came together, and were confounded, because that every man heard them speak in his own language. And they were all amazed and marvelled, saying one to another, Behold, are

not all these which speak Galilaeans? And how hear we every man in our own tongue, wherein we were born?"

Things that never happened before came to be, everyone speaking in an unknown tongues. It was a miracle that all could see, this miracle still happens. Many believers are receiving the gifts of the Holy Spirit, some are receiving the gift of interpreting a language they do not learn or understand naturally. By the outpouring of the Holy Spirit, their gifts are activated and they will begin to speak in tongues, interpreting other languages, see visions, prophecies and even performed miracles. These things are as a result of the miracle working God.

PRAYER OF BRETHREN

The Holy Bible made us to know how Peter was set free by the supplication of the believers.

Acts 12:5-12 KJV

"Peter therefore was kept in prison: but prayer was made without ceasing of the church unto God for him. And when Herod would have brought him forth, the same night Peter was sleeping between two soldiers, bound with two chains: and the keepers before the door kept the prison. And, behold, the angel of the Lord came upon him, and a light shined in the prison: and he smote Peter on the side, and raised him up, saying, Arise up quickly. And his chains fell off from his hands. And the angel said unto him, Gird thyself, and bind on thy sandals. And so he did. And he saith unto him, Cast thy garment about thee, and follow me. And he went out, and followed him; and wist not that it was true which was done by the angel; but thought he saw a vision. When they were past the first and the second ward, they came unto the iron gate that leadeth unto the city; which opened to them of his own accord: and they went out, and passed on through one

street; and forthwith the angel departed from him. And when Peter was come to himself, he said, Now I know of a surety, that the Lord hath sent his angel, and hath delivered me out of the hand of Herod, and from all the expectation of the people of the Jews. And when he had considered the thing, he came to the house of Mary the mother of John, whose surname was Mark; where many were gathered together praying."

Peter would have been killed but for the genuine and continuous prayer of the saints hence his release by God's angel. Peter was loosed from the prison, from untimely death and out of the city miraculously.

Prayer in accordance to the will of God, miracle happens. Pray today and you will receive your miracle, the Lord is near to answer your prayer.

A WISE COUNSEL TURNED USELESS

David was just like every other man on earth, an imperfect man who do fall into errors every now and then but it is the heart of repentance that made him a beloved of God. Once he realized his mistakes, he will genuinely repent and ask for forgiveness. It was during one of his errors that he committed a sin; killing Uriah after committing adultery with Uriah's wife. After the death of Uriah, he took Uriah's wife to be his and they both lived together in his palace. This Uriah's wife Bathsheba later became the mother of Solomon, the heir to the throne of David but during this error, David already made an enemy in Ahithopel. Ahithopel was the grandfather of Bathsheba, for she was the daughter of Eliam the son of Ahithopel. This means that it was the son-in-law of Ahithopel that David murdered, a person who was renowned for his angel-like counsel. He was the Counsel to the King himself.

2 Samuel 16:23KJV

"And the counsel of Ahithophel, which he counselled in those days, was as if a man had enquired at the oracle of God: so was all the

counsel of Ahithophel both with David and with Absalom."

Ahithopel had a grudge with David and a scores to settle with David's house for killing his son in law and taking in his granddaughter but he forgot that who God has forgiven is free from man's judgment. David repented and paid with the life of the unborn child Bathsheba first had for him through their immoral act. And it was still God's judgment that sword which is vengance did not depart from the house of David. For this God's judgment, many blood of David's children were spilled by vengance against each other. So Ahithopel had no right to intervene in God's punishment.

2 Samuel 16:20-22 KJV
Then said Absalom to Ahithophel, Give counsel among you what we shall do.

21 And Ahithophel said unto Absalom, Go in unto thy father's concubines, which he hath left to keep the house; and all Israel shall hear that thou art abhorred of thy father: then shall the hands of all that are with thee be strong.

22 So they spread Absalom a tent upon the top of the house; and Absalom went in unto his father's concubines in the sight of all Israel.

David on his own was suffering from the fear of been overthrowned and killed by his own son, he did not want to have to be in another fear of Ahithopel's bitter plot because he knew how much wisdom Ahithopel possessed.

2 Samuel 17:1-4 KJV

Moreover Ahithophel said unto Absalom, Let me now choose out twelve thousand men, and I will arise and pursue after David this night:

2 And I will come upon him while he is weary and weak handed, and will make him afraid: and all the people that are with him shall flee; and I will smite the king only:

3 And I will bring back all the people unto thee: the man whom thou seekest is as if all returned: so all the people shall be in peace.

4 And the saying pleased Absalom well, and all the elders of Israel.

David knew Ahithopel counsel was a gift from God but in this case, Ahithopel was using it for selfish and personal motive due to bitterness that has waged up in him hence David prayer to God to render Ahithope's counsel useless.

> *2 Samuel 17:6-14 KJV*
>
> *And when Hushai was come to Absalom, Absalom spake unto him, saying, Ahithophel hath spoken after this manner: shall we do after his saying? if not; speak thou.*
>
> *And Hushai said unto Absalom, The counsel that Ahithophel hath given is not good at this time.*
>
> *For, said Hushai, thou knowest thy father and his men, that they be mighty men, and they be chafed in their minds, as a bear robbed of her whelps in the field: and thy father is a man of war, and will not lodge with the people.*

Behold, he is hid now in some pit, or in some other place: and it will come to pass, when some of them be overthrown at the first, that whosoever heareth it will say, There is a slaughter among the people that follow Absalom.

And he also that is valiant, whose heart is as the heart of a lion, shall utterly melt: for all Israel knoweth that thy father is a mighty man, and they which be with him are valiant men.

Therefore I counsel that all Israel be generally gathered unto thee, from Dan even to Beersheba, as the sand that is by the sea for multitude; and that thou go to battle in thine own person.
So shall we come upon him in some place where he shall be found, and we will light upon him as the dew falleth on the ground:

and of him and of all the men that are with him there shall not be left so much as one. Moreover, if he be gotten into a city, then shall all Israel bring ropes to that city, and we will draw it into the river, until there be not one small stone found there.

And Absalom and all the men of Israel said, The counsel of Hushai the Archite is better than the counsel of Ahithophel. For the LORD had appointed to defeat the good counsel of Ahithophel, to the intent that the LORD might bring evil upon Absalom.

Everyman has his shortcomings, but the act to geniunely repent and go back to God is what makes one a believer. And once you are forgiving by God, then you are entitled to miraculous victory which David was priveledge to witness. He realized his mistake and repented, asked to be forgiving and he entered back into the miraculous yard of God. Just a prayer to God, the wise counsel of Ahithopel was rendered uesless.

> 2 Samuel 17:23 KJV
>
> *And when Ahithophel saw that his counsel was not followed, he saddled his ass, and arose, and gat him home to his house, to his city, and put his household in order, and hanged himself, and died, and was buried in the sepulchre of his father.*

Without David pronouncing judgment on Ahithopel, he hanged himself and David was left victorious.

VOMITTED OUT OF THE GRAVE

Jonah was a prophet of God but he served God with devotion and activities and not with love for he flee from God because of the message of repentance God sent him to Nineveh. Nineveh was a city in Azariah, a place inhabited by the people who did not serve God but idols. Theses people were full of evil deeds and they were enemies to the Israelites. Jonah wanted nothing to do with them as the usual tradition of the Jews but he failed to realised that God is the creator of all men throught the Word, either Jew or none Jew and God does not want His people to perish hence the message for repentance He sent Jonah. Despute their wicked ways, God still loved them but Jonah on his own part had no love for those people and do not want God to spare them, he wanted them to be destroyed so he decided to run away from God by going to the opposite direction of where God sent him. Jonah was sent to Nineveh but he sailed to Tarshish.

> *Jonah 1:1-12*
> *Now the word of the LORD came unto Jonahh the son of Amittai, saying,*

Arise, go to Nineveh, that great city, and cry against it; for their wickedness is come up before me.

But Jonahh rose up to flee unto Tarshish from the presence of the LORD, and went down to Joppa; and he found a ship going to Tarshish: so he paid the fare thereof, and went down into it, to go with them unto Tarshish from the presence of the LORD.
But the LORD sent out a great wind into the sea, and there was a mighty tempest in the sea, so that the ship was like to be broken.

Then the mariners were afraid, and cried every man unto his god, and cast forth the wares that were in the ship into the sea, to lighten it of them. But Jonahh was gone down into the sides of the ship; and he lay, and was fast asleep.

So the shipmaster came to him, and said unto him, What meanest thou, O sleeper? arise, call upon thy God, if so be that God will think upon us, that we perish not.

And they said every one to his fellow, Come, and let us cast lots, that we may know for whose cause this evil is upon us. So they cast lots, and the lot fell upon Jonahh.

Then said they unto him, Tell us, we pray thee, for whose cause this evil is upon us; What is thine occupation? and whence comest thou? what is thy country? and of what people art thou?

And he said unto them, I am an Hebrew; and I fear the LORD, the God of heaven, which hath made the sea and the dry land.

Then were the men exceedingly afraid, and said unto him. Why hast thou done this? For the men knew that he fled from the presence of the LORD, because he had told them.

Then said they unto him, What shall we do unto thee, that the sea may be calm unto us? for the sea wrought, and was tempestuous.
And he said unto them, Take me up, and cast me forth into the sea; so shall the sea be calm unto you: for I know that for my sake this great tempest is upon you.

Though Jonah delibrately committed disobedient by running away but one thing about God is that He is linient with us, He does not always deal with us according to our transgression because He knows that we are naive, if God was to be a man, many would have been destroyed. So God ordered a big fish to swallow Jonah up but not to kill or suffocate him.

Jonah 1:15-17 KJV

So they look up Jonah, and cast him forth into the sea: and the sea ceased from her raging.

16 Then the men feared the LORD exceedingly, and offered a sacrifice unto the LORD, and made vows.

17 Now the LORD had prepared a great fish to swallow up Jonahh. And Jonah was in the belly of the fish three days and three nights.

Jonah stayed in the belly of the fish was a miracle on its own because we can say that he was literally dead for three days but in Jonah's grave which is the belly of the fish, Jonah prayed to God.

Jonah 2:1-10

Then Jonahh prayed unto the LORD his God out of the fish's belly,

And said, I cried by reason of mine affliction unto the LORD, and he heard me; out of the belly of hell cried I, and thou heardest my voice.
For thou hadst cast me into the deep, in the midst of the seas; and the floods compassed me about: all thy billows and thy waves passed over me.

Then I said, I am cast out of thy sight; yet I will look again toward thy holy temple
The waters compassed me about, even to the soul: the depth closed me round about, the weeds were wrapped about my head.

I went down to the bottoms of the mountains; the earth with her bars was about me for ever: yet hast thou brought up my life from corruption, O LORD my God.

When my soul fainted within me I remembered the LORD: and my prayer came in unto thee, into thine holy temple.

They that observe lying vanities forsake their own mercy.

But I will sacrifice unto thee with the voice of thanksgiving; I will pay that that I have vowed. Salvation is of the LORD.

And the LORD spake unto the fish, and it vomited out Jonahh upon the dry land.

God is a merciful God, a mysterious God and His ways are full of wonders. Jonah cried to God for a miracle of another opportunity to worship at

God's temple and God answered his prayer. Prayer is a powerful tool in the working of miracle and by prayer, the miraculous is bound to happen.

Also, Hannah poured out her bitterness in the temple through her silent supplication.

> 1 Samuel 1:10
> *And she was in bitterness of soul, and prayed unto the LORD, and wept sore.*
> *And she vowed a vow, and said, O LORD of hosts, if thou wilt indeed look on the affliction of thine handmaid, and remember me, and not forget thine handmaid, but wilt give unto thine handmaid a man child, then I will give him unto the LORD all the days of his life, and there shall no razor come upon his head.*

And it came to pass, as she continued praying before the LORD, that Eli marked her mouth.

Now Hannah, she spake in her heart; only her lips moved, but her voice was not heard: therefore Eli thought she had been drunken.

And Eli said unto her, How long wilt thou be drunken? put away thy wine from thee.

And Hannah answered and said, No, my lord, I am a woman of a sorrowful spirit: I have drunk neither wine nor strong drink, but have poured out my soul before the LORD.
Count not thine handmaid for a daughter of Belial: for out of the abundance of my complaint and grief have I spoken hitherto.

Then Eli answered and said, Go in peace: and the God of Israel grant thee thy petition that thou hast asked of him.

And she said, Let thine handmaid find grace in thy sight. So the woman went her way, and did eat, and her countenance was no more sad.

And they rose up in the morning early, and worshipped before the LORD, and returned, and came to their house to Ramah: and Elkanah knew Hannah his wife; and the LORD remembered her.

Wherefore it came to pass, when the time was come about after Hannah had conceived, that she bare a son, and called his name Samuel, saying, Because I have asked him of the LORD.

She realized that it is only God that can intervene in her situation, the Priest did not understand her plight but God understood her.

Once you realized that God is your final solution you will surely receive a miracle like Hannah. Hannah succumb to God and she received her miracle.

CHAPTER SIX

CHANNEL OF THANKSGIVING

The easiest way to get a miracle is by thanksgiving, a thankful heart that is full of praise and worship shows how grateful such person is. Thanksgiving is a key to the heavenly realm, when you pray God send down His angels but when you sing His praises for His benevolent nature He shows towards you or just thank Him for His existence in your life. Before you know it, He will come down Himself and wherever God is, He is there with Hosts of Heaven. Where God is, Jesus the Son is there and so is the Holy Spirit. Where God is, miracle must surely happen because sickness, suffering, bondage and all agents of darkness cannot stay in where God is. He is a God of Holiness and Perfection so imperfect cannot abode with Him.

BONDAGE TO FREEDOM

Acts 16:25-26 KJV

"And at midnight Paul and Silas prayed, and sang praises unto God: and the prisoners heard them. And suddenly there was a great earthquake, so that the foundations of the prison were shaken: and immediately all the doors were opened, and every one's bands were loosed."

These disciples never asked to be set free, their praising of God did not have hidden agenda or interior motives. They simply were praising God for the grace showered on them to be acknowledged as God's people, they were glad to be recognized as Jesus Christ disciples, they were grateful to be arrested for Christ's sake for preaching the gospel and doing the work of the Father. They never asked for anything in return but God in return visited them. Bible recorded that the prison was shaken to the foundation just like when God descended on Mount Sinai

> *Exodus 19:16-18 KJV*
>
> *"And it came to pass on the third day in the morning, that there were thunders and lightnings, and a thick cloud upon the mount, and the voice of the trumpet exceeding loud; so that all the people that was in the camp trembled. And Moses brought forth the people out of the camp to meet with God; and they stood at the nether part of the mount. And mount Sinai was altogether on a smoke, because the Lord descended upon it in fire: and the smoke thereof ascended as the smoke of a furnace, and the whole mount quaked greatly."*

Likewise, by the descending of the Heaven, not only was it felt by the disciples but by everyone in the prison cell. All were let loose, freed and relieved of their burdens. Where God is, no shackles can hold us down.

VICTORY WITHOUT A FIGHT

When you praise God for His works, signs and wonders are sure to happen. Thanksgiving is a miraculous weapon you can use to fight and won without lifting a finger.

2 Chronicles 20:1-4 KJV

"It came to pass after this also, that the children of Moab, and the children of Ammon, and with them other beside the Ammonites, came against Jehoshaphat to battle. Then there came some that told Jehoshaphat, saying, There cometh a great multitude against thee from beyond the sea on this side Syria; and, behold, they be in Hazazon–tamar, which is En–gedi. And Jehoshaphat feared, and set himself to seek the Lord, and proclaimed a fast throughout

all Judah. And Judah gathered themselves together, to ask help of the Lord: even out of all the cities of Judah they came to seek the Lord."

Jehoshaphat and his army were outnumbered by the enemies, the Israelites lost hope in the battle on winning on their own but with hope in God and thanksgiving as a tool, the table turned.

2 Chronicles 20:19-24 KJV
"And the Levites, of the children of the Kohathites, and of the children of the Korhites, stood up to praise the Lord God of Israel with a loud voice on high. And they rose early in the morning, and went forth into the wilderness of Tekoa: and as they went forth, Jehoshaphat stood and said, Hear me, O Judah, and ye inhabitants of Jerusalem; Believe in the Lord your God, so shall ye be established; believe his prophets, so shall ye prosper. And when he had consulted with the people, he appointed

singers unto the Lord, and that should praise the beauty of holiness, as they went out before the army, and to say, Praise the Lord; for his mercy endureth for ever. And when they began to sing and to praise, the Lord set ambushments against the children of Ammon, Moab, and mount Seir, which were come against Judah; and they were smitten."

"For the children of Ammon and Moab stood up against the inhabitants of mount Seir, utterly to slay and destroy them: and when they had made an end of the inhabitants of Seir, every one helped to destroy another. And when Judah came toward the watch tower in the wilderness, they looked unto the multitude, and, behold, they were dead bodies fallen to the earth, and none escaped."

They never lift a finger to fight the enemy but miraculously, they won the battle through thanksgiving from their heart. No wonder David said in his Psalms

Psalms 103:1-6 KJV

"Bless the Lord, O my soul: and all that is within me, bless his holy name. Bless the Lord, O my soul, and forget not all his benefits: Who forgiveth all thine iniquities; who healeth all thy diseases; Who redeemeth thy life from destruction; who crowneth thee with lovingkindness and tender mercies; Who satisfieth thy mouth with good things; so that thy youth is renewed like the eagle's. The Lord executeth righteousness and judgment for all that are oppressed'.

Thanksgiving from the heart produces stress free miracle.

CHAPTER SEVEN

GETTING THE RESULT

Looking at biblical miracles, we can see that they differ from one another but they all come from one source. Typology of miracle is the key to miracle but applying it rightly determines the result.

In this chapter, we will be going through process of miracle for a desired result. To get a miracle these processes have to be carried out.

- Intimacy with Jesus Christ

The Bible says in Romans 3:23KJV "For all have sinned, and come short of the glory of God;"

God knows that we are sinners, none is perfect since we have inherited sin from Adam and Eve, we ourselves daily sin and it is only by the blood of Jesus Christ we can be made clean.

Romans 3:24-26 KJV

Being justified freely by his grace through the redemption that is in Christ Jesus:

Whom God hath set forth to be a propitiation through faith in his blood, to declare his righteousness for the remission of sins that are past, through the forbearance of God;

To declare, I say, at this time his righteousness: that he might be just, and the justifier of him which believeth in Jesus.

Jesus Christ purposedly came down for the salvation of all, He willingly poured His blood for us so that we can be saved.

Matthew 23:27-28
And he took the cup, and gave thanks, and gave it to them, saying, Drink ye all of it;

> *For this is my blood of the new testament, which is shed for many for the remission of sins.*

For a miracle to take place in your life, you need Jesus Christ. Gone are the days when anyone can recieve grace irrespective of accepting Jesus or not.

> *John 14:6*
>
> *" Jesus saith unto him, I am the way, the truth, and the life: no man cometh unto the Father, but by me."*

We are in the despensation of The Son, only through Him can we receive from The Father. The word of God says

> *Phillippians 2:9-11*
>
> *Wherefore God also hath highly exalted him, and given him a name which is above every name:*

10 That at the name of Jesus every knee should bow, of things in heaven, and things in earth, and things under the earth;

And that every tongue should confess that Jesus Christ is Lord, to the glory of God the Father.

This name can only be used when you are acquited with Jesus Christ. You have to know Jesus Christ personally by accepting Him as your Lord and Saviour that is when the name can be powerful when you command with it. For an unrepentant sinner to use the name Jesus Christ to command is just like the sons of Sceva

Acts 9:11-16 KJV
11 And God wrought special miracles by the hands of Paul:

12 So that from his body were brought unto the sick handkerchiefs or aprons, and the diseases departed from them, and the evil spirits went out of them.

13 Then certain of the vagabond Jews, exorcists, took upon them to call over them which had evil spirits the name of the LORD Jesus, saying, We adjure you by Jesus whom Paul preacheth.

14 And there were seven sons of one Sceva, a Jew, and chief of the priests, which did so.

15 And the evil spirit answered and said, Jesus I know, and Paul I know; but who are ye?
16 And the man in whom the evil spirit was leaped on them, and overcame them, and

prevailed against them, so that they fled out of that house naked and wounded.

But a repentant sinner who have been accepted by Jesus Christ is now God's person because through Jesus Christ, he has been accepted into God's fold. If you are searching for a miracle today, why not repent from your past wrong and crooked ways to have a right way of Jesus Christ. Genuine repentance is what God wants.

> *Acys 3:19 KJV*
> *19 Repent ye therefore, and be converted, that your sins may be blotted out, when the times of refreshing shall come from the presence of the Lord.*

Ask God to forgive you your sin and accept you into his fold for the sake of the blood of Jesus Christ He poured on the cross of Calvary.

If you are truely sorry, God is ready to accept you today and this is the begining of your journey to miracle.

- Justification, Salvation, Sanctificatuon and Grace

For a repentance to take place, you must have heard the word of the goapel and had an encounter with the Master and be chose by Him for redemption

> *Romana 8:30 KJV*
> *30 Moreover whom he did predestinate, them he also called: and whom he called, them he also justified: and whom he justified, them he also glorified.*

For yor heart to be touched, you have been singled out. When you repent from your sin, you will be saved by the blood of the lamb which is Jesus Christ, automatically you are justified to be called son of God.

Roman 1:12-14 KJV

But as many as received him, to them gave he power to become the sons of God, even to them that believe on his name:

Which were born, not of blood, nor of the will of the flesh, nor of the will of man, but of God.

And the Word was made flesh, and dwelt among us, (and we beheld his glory, the glory as of the only begotten of the Father,) full of grace and truth.

Salvation bring His blood brings you to your right which is justification in Christ to be among the Saved and you will become a sanctified versel, soul and a new being in Christ.

2 Corinthians 5:17-20 KJV

Therefore if any man be in Christ, he is a new creature: old things are passed away; behold, all things are become new.

And all things are of God, who hath reconciled us to himself by Jesus Christ, and hath given to us the ministry of reconciliation;

To wit, that God was in Christ, reconciling the world unto himself, not imputing their trespasses unto them; and hath committed unto us the word of reconciliation.

Now then we are ambassadors for Christ, as though God did beseech you by us: we pray you in Christ's stead, be ye reconciled to God.
You are no more the old sinner but a new clean person in Christ who has recieved salvation from Salvation from the Word, spuritually just to be in

the God's fold and has been dusted and clean to become a new being then giving a Grace to new life in Christ. The grace to be His, the grace to call Him Abba, the grace to recieve the Holy Spirit who is the comforter, the grace to fellowship with Him and the grace to walk over all power of darkness.

> *Luke 10:19-20 KJV*
>
> *Behold, I give unto you power to tread on serpents and scorpions, and over all the power of the enemy: and nothing shall by any means hurt you.*
>
> *Notwithstanding in this rejoice not, that the spirits are subject unto you; but rather rejoice, because your names are written in heaven.*

You are now in Christ after passing through all the above steps, Jesus Christ is in you. He lives in you through the indwelling of the Holy Spirit so you are now a miracle carrier. You already have the miracle in you

Begin to study the word of God *Joshua 1:8 " 8 This book of the law shall not depart out of thy mouth; but thou shalt meditate therein day and night, that thou mayest observe to do according to all that is written therein: for then thou shalt make thy way prosperous, and then thou shalt have good success."*

Studying the Bible will give you the right key, the right verse to use for a particular battle you are in. It will teach and reveal what to do for you, things you do not know that can work.

In the next and last chapter, I will discuss how to activate the miracle with real life experince I witnessed during the course of my ministration, deliverance session and spiritual impartation. By then you will understand more that working in Spirit of God is nothing but a miracle.

CHAPTER EIGHT

ACTIVATING THE MIRACLE

Remember in the last chapter, I talked about getting the miracle in you and steps you have to take. After getting this miracle, you need to activate it to make it work. Many people have the miracle in then but few make use of it. Most are unaware of what they carry and it remain in them unsed.

Activation if the miracle involves some steps also you have to take. Carefully study the steps and you will be amazed with the result you will get.

- Faith

Matthew 17:20 KJV.

20 And Jesus said unto them, Because of your unbelief: for verily I say unto you, If ye have faith as a grain of mustard seed, ye shall say unto this mountain, Remove hence to yonder place; and it shall remove; and nothing shall be impossible unto you.

Prayer without faith is meaningless, also praise without having faith in God is just a waste of time.

James 1:6 – 8 KJV
But let him ask in faith, nothing wavering. For he that wavereth is like a wave of the sea driven with the wind and tossed.

For let not that man think that he shall receive any thing of the Lord.

A double minded man is unstable in all his ways.

The first time I conducted a spiritual impartation session for a minister, I did it based on faith in the word of God. God told me that spiritual impartation, deliverance and Word are what the ministry He gave us is into. I do not know much about the person I was to pray for, neither do I know how the spirit of God will manifest, I do not even know where He is going to come from but all I know is that I must help push out the gifts of the Holy Spirit already deposited in the minister in order for her to be able to use it for the expansion of the kingdom of God. I did not have a power of my own other than the power of God giving to me by the Holy Spirit. On the part of the minister, she was scared, yes she may be a minister in the face of the congregation but she has fears. Fear of the unknown, fear of failing just like me, fear of 'Can I Do It'; this statement is problematic to a new believer when in the path of the miraculous. The devil will keep bringing it up for you to doubt the power of God, yours is not to ask if you can do it because on your own you can not, but 'Can God Do It' and the answer is always Yes He Can Do It for there is nothing impossible with God. Just have faith in God, chaste doubt away so that you can be free of fear. Once you fear, nothing will happen.

When you praise or pray to God, do so with the mind that your prayer is answered already. Do so with sureness of heart, free of doubt.

> *Mark 11:24*
> *24 Therefore I say unto you, What things soever ye desire, when ye pray, believe that ye receive them, and ye shall have them.*

When you accept Jesus Christ as your Lord and Saviour, you do so because you know that He can save you, likewise when you pray, praise or command a thing to happen, do so with certainty. With trust you have in God who answers his children's prayer.

Matthew 7:7-11 KJV

7 Ask, and it shall be given you; seek, and ye shall find; knock, and it shall be opened unto you:

8 For every one that asketh receiveth; and he that seeketh findeth; and to him that knocketh it shall be opened.

9 Or what man is there of you, whom if his son ask bread, will he give him a stone?

10 Or if he ask a fish, will he give him a serpent?

11 If ye then, beingevil, know how to give good gifts unto your children, how much more shall your Father which is in heaven give good things to them that ask him?

Boldness is a fruit of faith, you do not faint when commanding a sickness or a demon to flee, you have to speak with the authority God as placed in your mouth. Immediately you are in Christ, Holy Spirit will begin to reside in you and He will come with both His fruits and gifts. The manifestation of His gifts are the miraculous works of the Holy Spirit but you have to activate it with the faith you have in God that He never lies. Jesus Christ said we have bewn giving power to trample over serpent and scorpionsbwhich means that tiu have being giving authority over the hosts of darkness with their fruits which are poverty, sorrow, sickness, barreness and all sorts of unpleasant things. To chaste them out, you have to be bold, stand your ground whenever you hear a voice or thought that says you can not do it.

For someone speaking in tongues for the first time, the first thing you will hear is that 'You Are Speaking Rubbish', whenever you hear that, know that the devil is speaking and trying to distract you. Do not stop what you are saying but first the tongue

you are speaking must come from God, that is it must come upon you by, the Holy Spirit, through His inspiration and not a tongue that you formed yourself or hear some person speak when you think you can copy the person. No, that is a man made tongue. Tongues from the Holy Spirit will come upon you through the inspiration of the Holy Spirit which will be felt all over your body, from you hair, down to your toes. You will feel the breeze and touch on your body, you will know that something has come upon you, and your tongue will change .
During this process, you will feel like opening your eyes, trying to draw back from the unknown and you will feel electrified being circulated through your vein. Relax your body and let the Holy Spirit take control, have faith in Him and He will pefect His work.

Both spiritual impartation, deliverance and healing takes the same way to work but it is the Holy Spirit that decide which one to take place. He works according to the need of the reciever, all is needeed is faith to make it work.

God is our Father throught the remitance of the blood of Jesus, when you ask in Jesus name, your request will be answered.

- Courage and Confidence

A weak man can not caste out devil for satan moves with fear. Where there is fear in man, miracle can not be performed. Faith, couragrand hundred percent confidence in God are things needed to defeat devil. If he sense that you fear him, he will scare you the more.

During a journey in the miraculous, you will face antagonism from both spiritual and physical. People you know and even working with will try to discourage you but you have to stay courageous. Miraculous journey is warfare and you can only conquer through your faith in the protection of God, courage in His ability to overcome, that is when things can happen. It was courage and faith that kept me going during my early stage in the ministry when we would spend like three, five or seven hours on a spiritual impartation for just single person. Then it was myself, my husband, my son, and 3 others minister in our ministry THESEWHO , I did not yet know that I can singlehandedly conduct a session and even with the six and seven of us and me taking the lead, we still spend several hours on a person. As we would be praying in tongues, I would be checking from time to time if the prayer is actually working, my faith then was low but I got courage from the response I got, the shaking of the body alone encouraged me and others to keep praying because we knew that we are connected to the spiritual realm of God.

When you are new in the journey, as man doubt will come ones in a while, you will argue within yourself, but continue in your prayer or worship which ever one you are comfortable with, mine is praying in tongue no minding if I understand all of what am sating or little of it, or I do not know at all but I know that the tongue is an inspiration from the Holy Spirit I will continue saying it. Little by little, it will begin to work for both the receiver and myself that is working for the miraculous. The more I work, the more I am building myself up. From there, the time began to reduce and now both deliverance and spiritual impartation may not be up to thirty minutes altogether and I am still a work in progress. The more your faith and courage in God is, the more effective the spiritual power God has deposited in you through the spiritual gifts of the Holy Spirit will work.

Also, when the hosts of heaven, God's angels see fear in you, they will stay back not lifting a finger to assist you because you are unsure of yourself and in the name of Jesus Christ you command with. Infact you are not certain if God can really defeat the darkness. Heaven needs a courageous and confident person, strongin faith who can face the power of darkness and not an already defeated soldier.

> *Hebrew 11:6 KJV*
>
> *6 But without faith it is impossible to please him: for he that cometh to God must believe that he is, and that he is a rewarder of them that diligently seek him.*

When you are strong in faith, bold and certain of victory, call on the ne of Jesus Christ and you will see the result you will get. With confident in Him miracle is sure to happen.

- Prayer and Fasting

For your faith and courage to work for the miraculous, you must fast and pray continueously.

Matthew 17:15-21KJV

15 Lord, have mercy on my son: for he is lunatick, and sore vexed: for ofttimes he falleth into the fire, and oft into the water.

16 And I brought him to thy disciples, and they could not cure him.

17 Then Jesus answered and said, O faithless and perverse generation, how long shall I be with you? how long shall I suffer you? bring him hither to me.

18 And Jesus rebuked the devil; and he departed out of him: and the child was cured from that very hour.

19 Then came the disciples to Jesus apart, and said, Why could not we cast him out?

20 And Jesus said unto them, Because of your unbelief: for verily I say unto you, If ye have faith as a grain of mustard seed, ye shall say unto this mountain, Remove hence to yonder place; and it shall remove; and nothing shall be impossible unto you.

21 Howbeit this kind goeth not out but by prayer and fasting.

You are not asked to fast for a whole year or a whole month without eating a balance diet. For you to perform miracle you have to have the full power of the Holy Spirit. The power of the Holy Spirit do not start working in you the moment He touches you. The disciples in the upper room where speaking in an unknown languages when the Holy Spirit descended on them, but do not forget that they have been working and moving with Jesus Christ for three and half years. They were Jews which grew up with Judahism as religion, they had build themselves up to the level of receiving the Holy Spirit. In the upper room, they were there to fast, pray and wait for the promise of the Father which is the Holy Spirit so they were ready for the outpouring.

Likewise, Cornelius may be refered to as a gentile but fasting and prayer were not new to him and his household. They were familiar with fasting and prayer, all they needed was the true Word of Gpd whoch is obedient to the call of the gospel and recieve salvation, when they did it resulted in the baptism of the Holy Spirit.

If you want to loose and bound the spirit of darkness, you have to deny yourself of delicious meal at times. You may not be used to fasting, find a day to set apart for prayer and fasting. Fasting without prayer at intervals can not be effective, it will be just a hunger strike. If you have a health issue, you can go on a white fasting which you feed on fruits only, when your sugar level is too low then supplement it with little malt drink or something to supplement. Fasting does not kill if it is oberserved with wisdom.

By building yourself up with fasting and prayer, little by little you will begin to feel the Holy Spirit building up in you. Remember that Rome was not build in a day, so do not expect to start raising the dead on the first day of your fast. Continuous fasting and prayer coupled with the inclination of your heart if God wishes, you will be giving the gift of miracle.

> *1 Corinthians 12:7-11KJV*
> *7 But the manifestation of the Spirit is given to every man to profit withal.*
>
> *8 For to one is given by the Spirit the word of wisdom; to another the word of knowledge by the same Spirit;*

9 To another faith by the same Spirit; to another the gifts of healing by the same Spirit;

10 To another the working of miracles; to another prophecy; to another discerning of spirits; to another divers kinds of tongues; to another the interpretation of tongues:

11 But all these worketh that one and the selfsame Spirit, dividing to every man severally as he will.

These gifts are giving to man based on how you can handle each. If God sees that you want the gifts only to exploit people for your personal interest, it will not be giving.

Acts 8:14-23KJV

14 Now when the apostles which were at Jerusalem heard that Samaria had received the word of God, they sent unto them Peter and John:

15 Who, when they were come down, prayed for them, that they might receive the Holy Ghost:

16 (For as yet he was fallen upon none of them: only they were baptized in the name of the Lord Jesus.)

17 Then laid they their hands on them, and they received the Holy Ghost.

18 And when Simon saw that through laying on of the apostles' hands the Holy Ghost was given, he offered them money,

***19** Saying, Give me also this power, that on whomsoever I lay hands, he may receive the Holy Ghost.*
***20** But Peter said unto him, Thy money perish with thee, because thou hast thought that the gift of God may be purchased with money.*

***21** Thou hast neither part nor lot in this matter: for thy heart is not right in the sight of God.*

***22** Repent therefore of this thy wickedness, and pray God, if perhaps the thought of thine heart may be forgiven thee.*

***23** For I perceive that thou art in the gall of bitterness, and in the bond of iniquity.*

Gifts of God are to be used to bless others and not to glorify ourselves. A gift can be released to you at a time and you may be giving all if God pleases.

What is important is to use it for God according to His way and He will bless you with more.

> Matthew 25:14-28 KJV
>
> *14 For the kingdom of heaven is as a man travelling into a far country, who called his own servants, and delivered unto them his goods.*
>
> *15 And unto one he gave five talents, to another two, and to another one; to every man according to his several ability; and straightway took his journey.*
>
> *16 Then he that had received the five talents went and traded with the same, and made them other five talents.*
>
> *17 And likewise he that had received two, he also gained other two.*

18 But he that had received one went and digged in the earth, and hid his lord's money.

19 After a long time the lord of those servants cometh, and reckoneth with them
20 And so he that had received five talents came and brought other five talents, saying, Lord, thou deliveredst unto me five talents: behold, I have gained beside them five talents more.

21 His lord said unto him, Well done, thou good and faithful servant: thou hast been faithful over a few things, I will make thee ruler over many things: enter thou into the joy of thy lord.

22 He also that had received two talents came and said, Lord, thou deliveredst unto me two talents: behold, I have gained two other talents beside them.

23 *His lord said unto him, Well done, good and faithful servant; thou hast been faithful over a few things, I will make thee ruler over many things: enter thou into the joy of thy lord.*

24 *Then he which had received the one talent came and said, Lord, I knew thee that thou art an hard man, reaping where thou hast not sown, and gathering where thou hast not strawed:*

25 *And I was afraid, and went and hid thy talent in the earth: lo, there thou hast that is thine.*

26 *His lord answered and said unto him, Thou wicked and slothful servant, thou knewest that I reap where I sowed not, and gather where I have not strawed:*

***27** Thou oughtest therefore to have put my money to the exchangers, and then at my coming I should have received mine own with usury.*

***28** Take therefore the talent from him, and give it unto him which hath ten talents.*

Through continueous prayer, fasting and activately working in the journey, you will be able to build up your faith, then the courage and confidence in you will become stronger. With these, no power of the darkness can hold you back and you will become a living miracle carrier.

Conclusion
Getting there do not mean you will always be there, if your faith deminish when you think you do not need to fast and pray anymore because you think you are the one performing the miracle, then you should know that Satan is at work. When you see

the sign, bind the devil ontime before he fails you. Do not allow the devil to derail you by telling you how powerful, special and important you are. Pride, lies and adultery are the biggest weapon devil uses in bring down minister of God. Always pray and read the word of God; the Bible for the renewal of your inner man.

I pray for you that as you do these, may God find it in His infinite mercy to give you the grace to fight to the finish and recieve your reward in heaven and life in eternal. Amen

About the Author

Gold-Idowu Bimpe is an Evangelist and a Teacher Of the gospel. Born in the mid 80s, to a Nigerian parents, Emmanuel and Christianah Ayekoloye. Blessed with prophetic gifts to minister effectively, build up ministers and discern spirit from one another. She wrote Overcoming Deceit and Arts of Miracle during her studies at Divine Blessing Bible College and Seminary, Lagos, Nigeria. She is the founder of The Seed Evangelical World Outreach, a ministry that deals in teaching the undiluted word of God, deliverance from the captivity of Satan, building up ministers for different denominations through spiritual impartation for the work of The Master in churches and reaching out to the less privileged especially the orphanage. Married to Pastor Idowu Olaniyi Ezekiel, they both run the ministry, and are blessed with 3 lovely kids Richard, David and Ebenezer.

Her hobbies are cooking, reading, music, researching and soccer. She loves to hear from her readers, feel free to write her on pastorgoldbimpe@gmail.com. Facebook is Bimpe Gold

WARE RESOURCES AND PUBLISHING

WE ARE AN ALL IN ONE, ONE STOP PUBLISHING COMPANY!!!!

W.R.P. is a modest but skillful and knowledgeable Christian Publishing Company. We specialize in getting authors into print. We embrace and guide each author like a member of our family. We treat you fairly and recognize the importance of building a lasting relationship with you as an author. Join us in the walk to promote prosperity along with the message of encouragement and peace. Be one of the authors we transform and prepare for the world of information and books.

FEEL FREE TO CONTACT US@

www.wareresources.com
1-888-469-4850 EXT. 2

http://www.facebook.com/pages/Ware-Resources-and-Publishing
Ware Resources and Publishing
You Start and Finish With Us!

www.ingramcontent.com/pod-product-compliance
Lightning Source LLC
Chambersburg PA
CBHW050237120526
44590CB00016B/2120